Sparkle's Kindness with Holiday Ant Fun

JANNA HOOK

Copyright © 2020 by Janna Hook.

ISBN-978-1-6485-8189-2

All rights reserved. No part of this book may be reproduced or transmitted in any form or by any means, electronic or mechanical, including photocopying, recording, or by any information storage and retrieval system, without permission in writing from the copyright owner.

The views expressed in this work are solely those of the author and do not necessarily reflect the views of the publisher, and the publisher hereby disclaims any responsibility for them.

Matchstick Literary
1-888-306-8885
orders@matchliterary.com

On a sunny bright day in the forest lived a family of Ants, and in that family lived a little ant named SPARKLE.

Sparkle loved to play and climb trees in the forest.

All day Sparkle and Ryhli climbed the tall trees with her new friends Amy, Bee, and Jed. The day was quiet windy, ALL the Ants were higher in the Tree, but Sparkle could see that the little Ant Bee was starting to lose her grip, because of the wind. Bee was hanging on by one hand. Sparkle grabbed Bee's hand pulled her up onto the branch. Sparkle gave Bee a hug to let her know she was safe now.

Bee told Sparkle THANK YOU, and that Sparkle was the KINDEST, Ant in the forest.

Soon Sparkle became known in the forest as the Super, Kindest, Hero Ant of all time

As Sparkle realized that her and Bee were safe, Sparkle said to Bee let's go home. Sparkle began to climb right down the tree then march home.

After a long march home Sparkle told her Mother, what had happened, that her little friend Bee was almost blown right off the tree branch she was on. Sparkle told her mother that she was worried that might happen to Bee again.

WHAT SHOULD A LITTLE ANT DO?

Bee marched home and was humming a song to herself.
Just what makes that little Bee Ant.
Think she can climb a very large tree.
Everyone knows an Ant can't hang onto to a large tree
Branch.
BUT!!!!
She's got great friends!!!
She's got great friends!!!
She's got crumb raspberry jam with her great friends. Any time Bee's feeling low, she just remembers her friends.
Now she's not feeling low anymore.

As Bee marched home singing her song. Bee came thru the door and called her mother Kambri.

Mom you should have seen what happened to me today. Bee's mother Kambri listened to Bee tell her all about the climbing tree, and how Sparkle helped her so she didn't fall. Kambri called over to talk to Rose. Kambri told Rose how WONDERFUL Sparkle is for saving

Bee from falling from the tree today.

Rose told Kambri that Sparkle would be happy to go climbing trees with Bee. That a group of friends all went together just for that reason. To keep the little Ants safe. OK said Ashli as long as Sparkle can be with Bee she can continue to climb Trees with Sparkle and the older group of friends.

Bee said GREAT, GREAT, GREAT!!!

Being a big girl is so fun and an adventure all it's own.
So many things to do and think about.

The next day, as Sparkle woke up she could see her sister Ryhli trying on spooky outfits, Sparkle jumped out of bed to ask Ryhli what she was doing?

Rhyli looked at her and said, "Halloween is in two days and you have to dress up in a costume and go around to all our neighbors with a bag and yell Trick or Treat and when they open the door they will give you a Fun Crumb,
it is so much fun!

One thing Sparkle don't go past our favorite climbing tree because all of the RED ANTS will be out too.
"What is RED ANT like"?, Sparkle asked.

"They are Ants like us, but they have big red pinchers on their face. I think it serves them when they want to carry food back to their houses. Total advantage over a black worker Ant, anyway the black worker ants like us are much stronger in other ways, because we don't have the pinchers to use to collect food. Still stay away from RED ANTS because some of the younger Red Ants use them to pinch us too!"

"Oh no, maybe I won't go out on Halloween!"

"Yes you should go, just stay close to home but no farther than our favorite climbing tree, and you will be fi ne. Besides we have gone that way marching a million times. What do you think I should wear Ryhli?"

"I know", Ryhli said. "Put this on and you can go as an Ant Ghost".

"Great idea, I will", said Sparkle. "I do look scary; no Red Ants will try to snap at me with this on!"

"Okay, then you are all set for a fun time on Halloween night this year!"

Sparkle's mom adds that she should go out early, so she would be home by dark and eating her Fun Crumbs.

"Great idea", said Sparkle. "Soon it is Halloween and it's time to get ready to go out".

Ryhli's friends Jack came over to pick her up, and now it's time for Sparkle to go out too.

Just like Ryhli said everyone came to the door with a bowl of Fun Crumbs!

"Thank you", Sparkle said as the fun crumbs fell into her bag.

Sparkle said. "This is the best Holiday EVER!"

"I will march faster to the next house!" And she did.

From house to house she went as fast as she could. She arrived at Ant Ashli's and Uncle Chuck's house.

And off she went to march home.

"WOW! This is a fun day!"

As Sparkle started marching home she began to hear whispering behind her so she started to walk faster and then a little faster until Sparkle was in a full run with all six legs running as fast as she could with her bag of Fun Crumbs.

She was almost home when she looked back and saw TWO RED ANTS SNAPPING at her.

"STOP! STOP!"

"WAIT! WAIT!", so she called out to Jed, Sparkle's friend.

Jed is a worker Ant who climbs trees with her and Ryhli. Jed heard Sparkle and gathered up all his worker ant friends.

They all ran out of the house and formed a line across the pathway. Sparkle could see Jed and his friends. As Sparkle ran by Jed he asked her if she was okay.

"Yes", said Sparkle. "I am just a little scared".

As the RED ANTS got closer, they could see a large line of worker Ants!!

And they came to a stop, just then the largest worker Ant James stepped out of the line and said, "You weren't going to try to scare a little Ant, were you?"

The two RED Ants dropped what was in their snappers, and said out of breath, "I didn't think we were going to make it. Sparkle sure can run fast!"

We kept yelling at her to STOP and WAIT that just made her run faster.

Redwood and I tried to pick up all the Fun Crumbs we could, that just made it hard to tell Sparkle that all her Fun Crumbs were falling out of her bag. She has a huge hole in the bottom of her bag.

You know how much the birds love Fun Crumbs! By morning, Sparkles Crumbs would have been eaten by all the birds in the Forest.

Redwood and I felt like that would have made Sparkle feel bad to lose all her Fun Crumbs on Halloween.

Just then, Sparkle looked down and there it was a huge hole in the bottom of her bag and all her Fun Crumbs were GONE.

Sparkle was overjoyed with the help he got from her new friends Redwood and Eric.

"Thank you both, so much! Would you like some Fun Crumbs for helping me?"

"Enjoy your Fun Crumbs! Goodnight. We will see you tomorrow; we all have a lot of marching to do!"

Sparkle ran into her house and told her mom and dad all that had happened.

That's when everybody sat down and started eating all their fun Crumbs, even mom and dad had some Fun Crumbs.

HALLOWEEN IS A FUN TIME OF A YEAR!

The very next day, bright and early Sparkle woke up to a wonderful new day of marching with James, Chad and C.J. Just as everyone came out of their houses to go marching. Everyone could see Redwood and Eric coming over to see Jed and everyone.

"Where are you going?" yelled Redwood.

"We are on our way to Farmer Joes Garden to check for food. Do you want to come?"

"Yes, we have never been there!" said Redwood.

"What are we going to find to make such a long trip?"

"It's the best place around to find winter storage food and Raspberries."

"Wow, let's go!" said Redwood.

Chad said, "Have you ever tried a Raspberry?"

Redwood said, "No, I don't think I have ever seen one, are they heavy?"

"Oh yes! Answered Chad. "We are the only ants strong enough to carry one. The only thing about a raspberry is it's round and rolls off our backs as soon as we take a step forward."

Redwood piped up and said, "I have a great idea!"

Chad and James said, "What's that Redwood?"

"If we all work together and use our skills, you can carry one on your back, Eric and I will hold onto it with our snappers. Keeping it steady on your back when you move forward."

"That would be so great that we all could enjoy a treat from Framer Joes Garden! Let's go Redwood! I can't wait to get there to see this wonderful garden!"

Red wood said, "Do you come here every year?"

"Yes, we do! And this year with your great idea, I think we will be successful in bringing back home a Raspberry for us and one for your family. Every year, at Thanksgiving time all Ant family's' get together to thank our Lord for all the blessings he gives us."

Redwood said, "Who is the Lord?"

"Jesus Christ", said James. "He created this whole Earth an all the food we eat. In remembrance, we want to have a Raspberry Crumb Cake!"

Redwood said, "That must be why the giants light up their houses to celebrate the Lord, Jesus Christ"

James said, "Yes! The next day after we have our Raspberry Crumb Cake all the lights will come on and glow beautiful colors for every creature to see all night long. It even at times lights up the night so it's not so dark in the Forrest. We love to see the lights every year! We better be on our way, we have a lot of work to do!"

Chad Ant yelled everyone, "Up and to the pathway!"

So off they all marched.

As they got close to the Farmer Joes, James yelled out, "Everyone stop and everyone hurried off of the pathway! Worker ants, remember to stay close together as you may know farmer Joe is a giant and we could get stepped on. So we all know that would be safe if we watch out for giants! On! So let's go."

Off they went into the Raspberry Patch. The ground was loaded with fresh raspberries. Chad and C.J layed down on the ground. James, Owen, Jack and Jed all pushed the Raspberry into place on Chad and C.J back. Once it was there, Redwood and Eric held it in place just like they planned.

Chad said, "Let's go slowly at first and we can pick up the pace later".

Just as they were leaving the farm, the Giant farmer Joe walked past and kept on walking.

Chad said, "I don't think he saw us. That was close!"

With a sigh of relief, everyone started to walk home again.

It was a very long trip with a heavy load when everyone got home they couldn't even speak.

Sparkle came to the door and could see a team of Ants coming and yelled to her mom and dad to see come out to see a large berry coming down the path with Chad and C.J. under it.

Rose, Sparkle's mom said, "Just in time! The Crumb cake is ready for the raspberry!"

Just as they got to the crumb cake, everyone realized what was meant to take a few hours took all day.

It was getting dark. Chad and C.J knew that they would not be able to go back to farmer Joes again that day. Chad and C.J rolled that raspberry off their back and Rose said, "What a blessing to have a big berry!".

Sparkle said, "Let's share this wonderful berry with Redwood and Eric's family. "Without them we would not have made it home with such a large prize!"

With little rest Sparkle, Chad, Eric and Redwood were off to gather all the families. For the first time ever they had a Raspberry Crumb Cake Feast!

Soon Redwood and Eric's family and friends gathered around the wonderful Raspberry Crumb Cake. Before they started to eat, Roger Sparkles dad said, "We need to thank our Lord for this fine treat". Everyone including the Red Ants lowered their heads. While Roger said a prayer of thanks to the Lord for this fine treat ended with Amen. Everyone looks up and said, "Let's eat!"

So they did.

Red and black ants all enjoyed the wonderful taste of Raspberries.

From that year, all the Ants came over to Sparkles house to enjoy the Raspberry Crumb Cake to thank the Lord Jesus Christ. Plus they brought over other great snacks too.

They all had a ton of food to eat and enjoy the new friends they had come to know and love. With all the food, and fun it was dark and the twinkling of the colorful light can be seen by all. One small act of kindness can change the WORLD.

EVEN AN ANTS WORLD!

This book is dedicated to my family.

With Special thanks to Artist Kylie Hachmi

www.ingramcontent.com/pod-product-compliance
Lightning Source LLC
Chambersburg PA
CBHW042251100526
44587CB00002B/102